Filet Crochet
Table Runners

In styles to complement every décor, these filet crochet runners add a light
and airy look to any surface. White bedspread weight cotton is the classic
choice, but they would also look amazing in brights or pastels.

3

6

10

14

18

22

25

27

LEISURE ARTS, INC. • Little Rock, Arkansas

WHAT IS FILET CROCHET?

Filet crochet is a popular form of lace that uses a combination of solid blocks and open spaces to create pictures, motifs and patterns. It's most commonly worked using cotton thread and a steel hook, but is sometimes used for afghans made with yarn. Most often, filet crochet is worked from a square-grid chart which greatly simplifies the instructions to complete a pattern.

HOW TO FOLLOW A CHART

On filet crochet charts, the blocks are represented by solid squares and the spaces are represented by open squares.

An open square on a chart indicates a space, which is formed by a chain 2 and a double crochet.

A solid square on a chart indicates a block, which is formed by 3 double crochets.

Some filet charts also include a lacet which is formed by a chain 2, a single crochet, an additional chain 2, and a double crochet.

Usually you will find a note instructing you to follow the chart from **right** to **left** when working **right** side rows and from **left** to **right** when working **wrong** side rows.
If a pattern is symmetrical, a note is not included since it doesn't matter which direction you follow the chart.
The pattern of blocks, spaces and lacets is easily worked by following a graphed chart. The following Basic Chart Stitches list all of the combinations necessary to complete any of the Table Runners in this book.

BASIC CHART STITCHES

BEGINNING SPACE OVER SPACE
Ch 5, turn; skip next ch-2 sp, dc in next dc.

SPACE OVER SPACE
Ch 2, skip next ch-2 sp, dc in next dc.

SPACE OVER BLOCK
Ch 2, skip next 2 dc, dc in next dc.

BLOCK OVER SPACE
2 Dc in next ch-2 sp, dc in next dc.

BLOCK OVER BLOCK
Dc in next 3 dc.

DOUBLE SPACE OVER 2 BLOCKS
Ch 5, skip next 5 dc, dc in next dc.

DOUBLE SPACE OVER 1 SPACE AND 1 BLOCK
Ch 5, skip next ch-2 sp and next 3 dc, dc in next dc.

LACET
Ch 3, skip next 2 sts, sc in next st, ch 3, skip next 2 sts, dc in next dc.

DOUBLE SPACE OVER LACET
Ch 5, skip next 2 ch-3 sps, dc in next dc.

2 BLOCKS OVER DOUBLE SPACE
Dc in next 5 chs and in next dc.

Note: To work any block or space combination over a double space, work in same manner.

Picket Fence

Shown on page 5.

◼◼◻◻ **EASY +**

Approximate Finished Size: 14¼" wide x 29½" long (36 cm x 75 cm)

GAUGE INFORMATION

20 dc and 10 rows = 2" (5 cm)
  9 spaces = 2" (5 cm) wide
Gauge Swatch: 2" (5 cm) square
Ch 22.
Row 1: Dc in fourth ch from hook
(3 skipped chs count as first dc) and
in each ch across: 20 dc.
Rows 2-10: Ch 3 **(counts as first dc)**,
turn; dc in next dc and in each dc
across.
Finish off.

STITCH GUIDE

🎥 TREBLE CROCHET
  (abbreviated tr)

★ YO twice, insert hook in sp
indicated, YO and pull up a loop
(4 loops on hook), (YO and draw
through 2 loops on hook) 3 times.

INSTRUCTIONS
BODY

Ch 146; place a marker in fifth ch from
hook for Border placement.

Row 1 (Right side)**:** Dc in eighth ch
from hook **(7 skipped chs count as
first dc plus ch 2 and 2 skipped chs)**,
★ ch 2, skip next 2 chs, dc in next
ch; repeat from ★ across: 48 dc and
47 ch-2 sps (47 spaces).

Note: Loop a short piece of thread
around any dc to mark Row 1 as **right**
side.

Row 2: Ch 5 **(counts as first dc plus
ch 2, now and throughout)**, turn;
skip next ch-2 sp, dc in next dc
(1 beginning space made), (ch 2,
skip next ch-2 sp, dc in next dc) 3
times **(3 spaces made)**, (2 dc in
next ch-2 sp, dc in next dc) 4 times
(4 blocks made), (work 3 spaces,
work 4 blocks) 5 times, work 4 spaces:
24 blocks and 23 spaces.

Row 3: Work beginning space, work
2 spaces, work 1 block, (ch 2, skip next
2 dc, dc in next dc) 4 times **(4 spaces
made)**, work 1 block, ★ work 1 space,
work 1 block, work 4 spaces, work
1 block; repeat from ★ 4 times
more, work 3 spaces: 35 spaces and
12 blocks.

Row 4: Work beginning space, work 1 space, work 1 block, (work 6 spaces, work 1 block) 6 times, work 2 spaces: 40 spaces and 7 blocks.

Row 5: Work beginning space, work 1 space, [dc in next 3 dc (**1 block made**)], (work 6 spaces, work 1 block) 6 times, work 2 spaces.

Rows 6-13: Follow chart.

Rows 14-133: Following chart, repeat Rows 14-19, 20 times.

Rows 134-141: Follow chart.

Do **not** finish off.

BORDER

Border is worked in spaces and in stitches around entire edge of Body.

Rnd 1 (Right side)**:** Ch 1, do **not** turn; working in top of dc at end of rows, sc in dc of first row (last dc of Row 141), † ch 10, skip first 3 sps, (sc in next dc, ch 10, skip next 3 sps) across †; 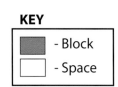 working in free loops of beginning ch *(Fig. 1, page 31)*, sc in first ch, ch 10, (skip next 3 sps, sc in next ch, ch 10) across to last 2 sps, skip last 2 sps, sc in marked ch; repeat from † to † once; working in dc on Row 141, sc in first dc, ch 10, [skip next 3 ch-2 sps, sc in next dc, ch 10] across to last 2 ch-2 sps, skip last 2 ch-2 sps; join with slip st to first sc: 126 sc and 126 ch-10 sps.

Rnd 2: Ch 1, sc in same st as joining, (3 hdc, 3 dc, 3 tr, 3 dc, 3 hdc) in next ch-10 sp, ★ sc in next sc, (3 hdc, 3 dc, 3 tr, 3 dc, 3 hdc) in next ch-10 sp; repeat from ★ around; join with slip st to first sc, finish off.

Wash and block Table Runner *(see Washing and Blocking, page 31)*.

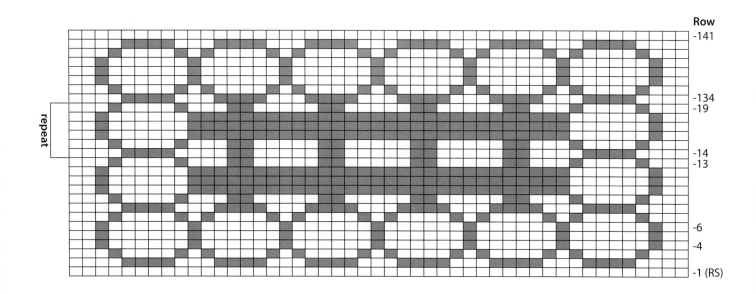

KEY

- ▨ - Block
- ☐ - Space

Chain Links

 **EASY +**

Approximate Finished Size: 14" wide x 31½" long (35.5 cm x 80 cm)

SHOPPING LIST

Thread

(Bedspread Weight)

[400 yards (366 meters) per ball]:

☐ 2 balls

Crochet Hook

☐ Steel, size 7 (1.65 mm)

or size needed for gauge

GAUGE INFORMATION

20 dc and 10 rows = 2" (5 cm)

9 spaces = 2" (5 cm) wide

Gauge Swatch: 2" (5 cm) square

Ch 22.

Row 1: Dc in fourth ch from hook

(3 skipped chs count as first dc) and

in each ch across: 20 dc.

Rows 2-10: Ch 3 **(counts as first dc)**,

turn; dc in next dc and in each dc

across.

Finish off.

STITCH GUIDE

2-TR CLUSTER (uses one sp)

★ YO twice, insert hook in sp

indicated, YO and pull up a loop, (YO

and draw through 2 loops on hook)

twice; repeat from ★ once **more**, YO

and draw through all 3 loops on hook.

3-TR CLUSTER (uses one sp)

★ YO twice, insert hook in sp

indicated, YO and pull up a loop, (YO

and draw through 2 loops on hook)

twice; repeat from ★ 2 times **more**, YO

and draw through all 4 loops on hook.

INSTRUCTIONS
BODY

Ch 152.

Row 1: Dc in eighth ch from hook **(7 skipped chs count as first dc plus ch 2 and 2 skipped chs)**, ★ ch 2, skip next 2 chs, dc in next ch; repeat from ★ across: 50 dc and 49 ch-2 sps (49 spaces).

Row 2 (Right side)**:** Ch 5 **(counts as first dc plus ch 2, now and throughout)**, turn; skip next ch-2 sp, dc in next dc **(1 beginning space made)**, (2 dc in next ch-2 sp, dc in next dc) 47 times **(47 blocks made)**, [ch 2, skip next ch-2 sp, dc in last dc **(1 space made)**]: 47 blocks and 2 spaces.

Note: Loop a short piece of thread around any dc to mark Row 2 as **right** side.

Row 3: Work beginning space, [dc in next 3 dc **(1 block made)**], (ch 2, skip next 2 dc, dc in next dc) 45 times **(45 spaces made)**, work 1 block, work 1 space: 47 spaces and 2 blocks.

Rows 4-31: Follow chart.

Rows 32-141: Following chart, work Rows 32-53, 5 times.

Rows 142-154: Follow chart.

Do **not** finish off.

BORDER

Border is worked in spaces and in stitches around entire edge of Body.

With **right** side facing and working in sps and in top of dc at end of rows, (slip st, ch 3, work 2-tr Cluster) in first sp, † [ch 4, skip next sp, sc in next dc, ch 4, skip next sp, work 3-tr Cluster in next sp] across, (ch 3, work 3-tr Cluster in same sp) twice †; working in sps and in free loops of beginning ch *(Fig. 1, page 31)*, [ch 4, skip next sp, sc in next ch, ch 4, skip next sp, work 3-tr Cluster in next sp] across, (ch 3, work 3-tr Cluster in same sp) twice; working in sps and in top of dc at end of rows, repeat from † to † once; working in sps and in dc on Row 154, [ch 4, skip next sp, sc in next dc, ch 4, skip next sp, work 3-tr Cluster in next sp] across, ch 3, work 3-tr Cluster in same sp, ch 3; join with slip st to top of first 2-tr Cluster, finish off.

Wash and block Table Runner *(see Washing and Blocking, page 31)*.

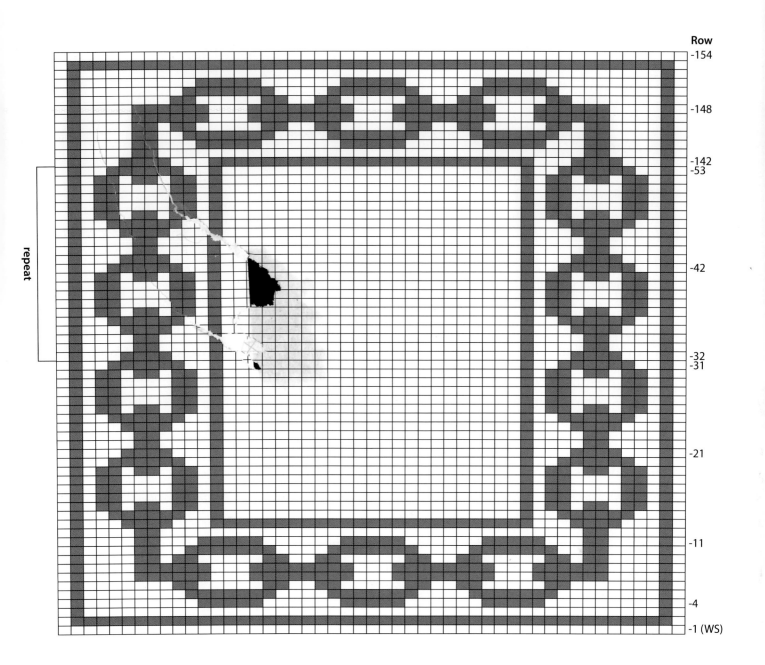

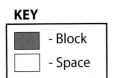

repeat

KEY

- Block

- Space

Diamonds

◼◼◻◻▷ **EASY +**

Approximate Finished Size: 13" wide x 28½" long (33 cm x 72.5 cm)

SHOPPING LIST

Thread
(Bedspread Weight)
[400 yards (366 meters) per ball]:
☐ 2 balls

Crochet Hook
☐ Steel, size 7 (1.65 mm)
or size needed for gauge

GAUGE INFORMATION
20 dc and 10 rows = 2" (5 cm)
     9 spaces = 2" (5 cm) wide
Gauge Swatch: 2" (5 cm) square
Ch 22.
Row 1: Dc in fourth ch from hook
(3 skipped chs count as first dc) and
in each ch across: 20 dc.
Rows 2-10: Ch 3 **(counts as first dc)**,
turn; dc in next dc and in each dc
across.
Finish off.

INSTRUCTIONS
BODY
Ch 146.

Row 1: Dc in eighth ch from h[___]
**(7 skipped chs count as first
ch 2 and 2 skipped chs),** ★
skip next 2 chs, dc in next c[_]
from ★ across: 48 dc and 47 ch-2 sps
(47 spaces).

Row 2 (Right side)**:** Ch 5 **(counts
as first dc plus ch 2, now and
throughout),** turn; skip next ch-2 sp,
dc in next dc **(1 beginning space
made),** (2 dc in next ch-2 sp, dc in
next dc) twice **(2 blocks made),**
(ch 2, skip next ch-2 sp, dc in next
dc) 11 times **(11 spaces made),**
work 1 block, (work 5 spaces, work
1 block) 3 times, work 11 spaces, work
2 blocks, [ch 2, skip next ch-2 sp, dc in
last dc **(1 space made)]:** 8 blocks and
39 spaces.

Note: Loop a short piece of thread
around any dc to mark Row 2 as **right
side.**

[Row] **3:** Work beginning space, [dc
[in ne]xt 6 dc **(2 blocks made)],** work
[_] spaces, work 1 block, [ch 2, skip
[n]ext 2 dc, dc in next dc **(1 space
made)],** work 1 block, work 5 spaces,
work 1 block, work 3 spaces, work
1 block, work 5 spaces, work 1 block,
work 1 space, work 1 block, work
10 spaces, work 2 blocks, work
1 space: 10 blocks and 37 spaces.

Rows 4-43: Follow chart, page 13.

Rows 44-131: Following chart, repeat
Rows 44-87 twice.

Rows 132-135: Follow chart.

Do **not** finish off.

BORDER

Border is worked in spaces and in stitches across each edge of Body.

FIRST LONG EDGE

First Point

Row 1 (Wrong side): Ch 3 (**counts as first dc, now and throughout**), do **not** turn; working in sps and in top of dc at end of rows, 2 dc in first sp, dc in next dc, (2 dc in next sp, dc in next dc) 6 times: 22 dc.

Row 2: Turn; slip st in first 4 dc, ch 3, dc in next 3 dc, ★ ch 2, skip next 2 dc, dc in next 4 dc; repeat from ★ once **more**, leave remaining 3 dc unworked: 12 dc and 2 ch-2 sps.

Row 3: Turn; slip st in first 4 dc, ch 3, 2 dc in next ch-2 sp, dc in next dc, ch 2, skip next 2 dc, dc in next dc, 2 dc in next ch-2 sp, dc in next dc, leave remaining 3 dc unworked: 8 dc and one ch-2 sp.

Row 4: Turn; slip st in first 4 dc, ch 3, 2 dc in next ch-2 sp, dc in next dc, leave remaining 3 dc unworked; finish off.

Second Point

Row 1: With **wrong** side facing, skip next sp from last Point made and join thread with slip st in next dc; ch 3, (2 dc in next sp, dc in next dc) 7 times: 22 dc.

Rows 2-4: Work same as First Point.

Remaining 15 Points

Work same as Second Point across entire edge.

FIRST SHORT EDGE

First Point

Row 1: With **wrong** side facing, 📹 working in free loops (*Fig. 1, page 31*) and in sps across beginning ch, join thread with slip st in first ch; ch 3, (2 dc in next sp, dc in next ch) 7 times: 22 dc.

Row 2: Turn; slip st in first 4 dc, ch 3, dc in next 3 dc, ★ ch 2, skip next 2 dc, dc in next 4 dc; repeat from ★ once **more**, leave remaining 3 dc unworked: 12 dc and 2 ch-2 sps.

Row 3: Turn; slip st in first 4 dc, ch 3, 2 dc in next ch-2 sp, dc in next dc, ch 2, skip next 2 dc, dc in next dc, 2 dc in next ch-2 sp, dc in next dc, leave remaining 3 dc unworked: 8 dc and one ch-2 sp.

Row 4: Turn; slip st in first 4 dc, ch 3, 2 dc in next ch-2 sp, dc in next dc, leave remaining 3 dc unworked; finish off.

Second Point

Row 1: With **wrong** side facing, skip next sp from last Point made and join thread with slip st in next st; ch 3, (2 dc in next sp, dc in next st) 7 times: 22 dc.

Rows 2-4: Work same as First Point.

Remaining 4 Points

Work same as Second Point across entire edge.

SECOND LONG EDGE

First Point

Row 1: With **wrong** side facing, working in sps and in top of dc at end of rows, join thread with slip st in first ch; ch 3, (2 dc in next sp, dc in next dc) 7 times: 22 dc.

Complete in same manner as First Long Edge, working Points across entire edge.

SECOND SHORT EDGE

First Point

Row 1: With **wrong** side facing, working in dc and in sps across Row 135, join thread with slip st in first dc; ch 3, (2 dc in next sp, dc in next st) 7 times: 22 dc.

Complete in same manner as First Short Edge, working Points across entire edge.

Wash and block Table Runner (*see Washing and Blocking, page 31*).

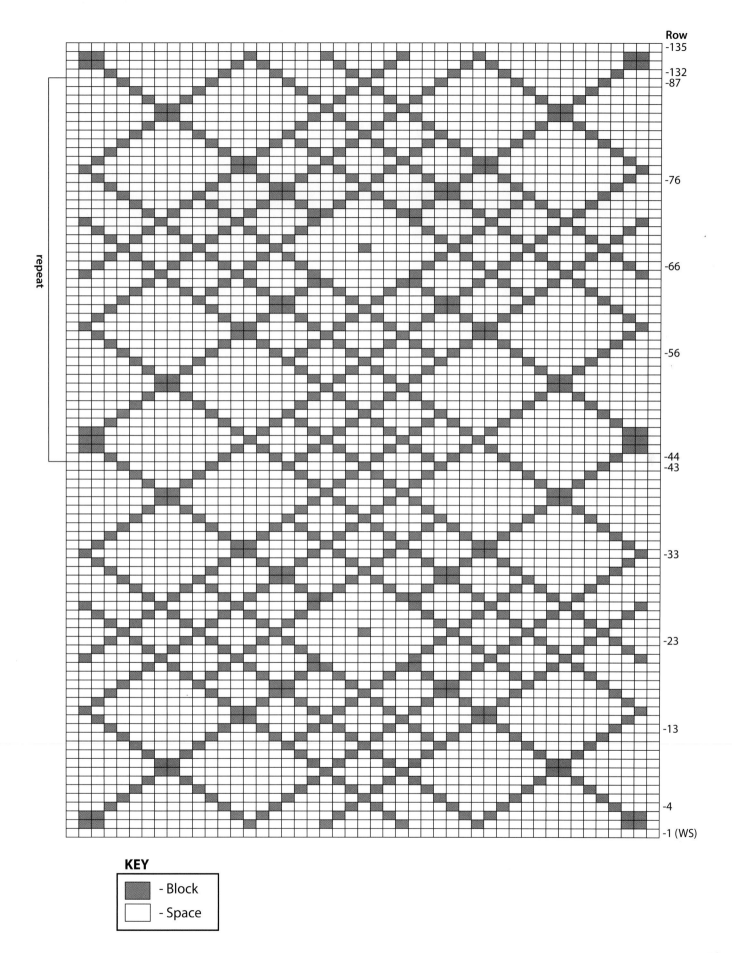

Row
-135
-132
-87

-76

-66

-56

repeat

-44
-43

-33

-23

-13

-4

-1 (WS)

KEY
- Block
- Space

Hearts & Lace

 **EASY +**

Approximate Finished Size: 13½" wide x 30" long (34.5 cm x 76 cm)

SHOPPING LIST

Thread

(Bedspread Weight) **LACE 0**

[400 yards (366 meters) per ball]:

☐ 2 balls

Crochet Hook

☐ Steel, size 7 (1.65 mm)

or size needed for gauge

GAUGE INFORMATION

20 dc and 10 rows = 2" (5 cm)

 9 spaces = 2" (5 cm) wide

Gauge Swatch: 2" (5 cm) square

Ch 22.

Row 1: Dc in fourth ch from hook

(3 skipped chs count as first dc) and

in each ch across: 20 dc.

Rows 2-10: Ch 3 **(counts as first dc)**,

turn; dc in next dc and in each dc

across.

Finish off.

INSTRUCTIONS
BODY

Ch 149.

Row 1 (Right side)**:** Dc in eighth ch

from hook **(7 skipped chs count as**

first dc plus ch 2 and 2 skipped chs),

★ ch 2, skip next 2 chs, dc in next

ch; repeat from ★ across: 49 dc and

48 ch-2 sps (48 spaces).

Note: Loop a short piece of thread

around any dc to mark Row 1 as **right**

side.

Row 2: Ch 5 **(counts as first dc plus**

ch 2, now and throughout), turn;

skip next ch-2 sp, dc in next dc

(1 beginning space made), (2 dc in

next ch-2 sp, dc in next dc) 46 times

(46 blocks made), [ch 2, skip next

ch-2 sp, dc in last dc **(1 space made)]:**

46 blocks and 2 spaces.

Row 3: Work beginning space, [dc

in next 6 dc **(2 blocks made)]**, (ch 2,

skip next 2 dc, dc in next dc) 13 times

(13 spaces made), [dc in next 3 dc

(1 block made)], work 14 spaces,

work 1 block, work 13 spaces, work

2 blocks, work 1 space: 42 spaces and

6 blocks.

Rows 4-12: Follow chart, page 17.

Row 13: Work beginning space, work

1 block, work 4 spaces, work 3 blocks,

work 2 spaces, work 1 block, (ch 5,

skip next 5 dc, dc in next dc) 12 times

(12 double spaces made), work

1 block, work 2 spaces, work 3 blocks,

work 4 spaces, work 1 block, work

1 space: 14 spaces, 12 double spaces,

and 10 blocks.

Row 14: Work beginning space, work 1 block, work 3 spaces, work 5 blocks, work 1 space, work 1 block, [ch 3, skip next 2 chs, sc in next ch, ch 3, skip next 2 chs, dc in next dc] 12 times **(12 lacets made)**, work 1 block, work 1 space, work 5 blocks, work 3 spaces, work 1 block, work 1 space: 14 blocks, 12 lacets, and 10 spaces.

Row 15: Work beginning space, work 1 block, work 2 spaces, work 6 blocks, work 1 space, work 1 block, (ch 5, skip next 2 ch-3 sps, dc in next dc) 12 times **(12 double spaces made)**, work 1 block, work 1 space, work 6 blocks, work 2 spaces, work 1 block, work 1 space: 16 blocks, 12 double spaces, and 8 spaces.

Rows 16-18: Follow chart.

Rows 19-130: Following chart, repeat Rows 19-32, 8 times.

Row 131: Work beginning space, work 1 block, work 2 spaces, work 6 blocks, work 1 space, work 1 block, work 2 double spaces, (ch 5, skip next ch-2 sps and next 3 dc, dc in next dc) 9 times **(9 double spaces made)**, work 1 double space, work 1 block, work 1 space, work 6 blocks, work 2 spaces, work 1 block, work 1 space: 16 blocks, 12 double spaces, and 8 spaces.

Rows 132-145: Follow chart.

Do **not** finish off.

BORDER

Border is worked in spaces around entire edge of Body.

Rnd 1 (Right side)**:** Ch 4 **(counts as first dc plus ch 1)**, do **not** turn; working in sps at end of rows, (dc, ch 1, dc) in first sp, ch 3, † ★ skip next sp, sc in next sp, ch 3, skip next sp, dc in next sp, (ch 1, dc in same sp) 4 times, ch 3; repeat from ★ across †; working in sps across beginning ch, sc in next sp, ch 3, skip next sp, dc in next sp, (ch 1, dc in same sp) 4 times, ch 3, [skip next sp, sc in next sp, ch 3, skip next sp, dc in next sp, (ch 1, dc in same sp) 4 times, ch 3] across; repeat from † to † once; working in sps on Row 145, sc in next ch-2 sp, ch 3, [skip next ch-2 sp, dc in next ch-2 sp, (ch 1, dc in same sp) 4 times, ch 3, skip next ch-2 sp, sc in next ch-2 sp, ch 3] across to last 2 ch-2 sps, skip next ch-2 sp, (dc, ch 1) twice in last ch-2 sp; join with slip st to first dc: 480 dc, 96 sc, and 576 sps.

Rnd 2: (Slip st, ch 1, sc) in next ch-1 sp, ch 3, sc in next ch-1 sp, ch 3, skip next ch-3 sp, sc in next sc, ch 3, ★ skip next ch-3 sp, (sc in next ch-1 sp, ch 3) 4 times, skip next ch-3 sp, sc in next sc, ch 3; repeat from ★ around to last 3 sps, skip next ch-3 sp, (sc in next ch-1 sp, ch 3) twice; join with slip st to first sc, finish off.

Wash and block Table Runner *(see Washing and Blocking, page 31)*.

repeat

KEY

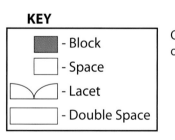

- Block
- Space
- Lacet
- Double Space

On **right** side rows, follow chart from **right** to **left**;
on **wrong** side rows, follow chart from **left** to **right**.

Sawtooth Stars

 **EASY +**

Approximate Finished Size: 13" wide x 28¼" long (33 cm x 72 cm)

GAUGE INFORMATION

20 dc and 10 rows = 2" (5 cm)

9 spaces = 2" (5 cm) wide

Gauge Swatch: 2" (5 cm) square

Ch 22.

Row 1: Dc in fourth ch from hook **(3 skipped chs count as first dc)** and in each ch across: 20 dc.

Rows 2-10: Ch 3 **(counts as first dc)**, turn; dc in next dc and in each dc across.

Finish off.

INSTRUCTIONS
BODY

Ch 152.

Row 1 (Right side)**:** Dc in eighth ch from hook **(7 skipped chs count as first dc plus ch 2 and 2 skipped chs)**, ★ ch 2, skip next 2 chs, dc in next ch; repeat from ★ across: 50 dc and 49 ch-2 sps (49 spaces).

Note: Loop a short piece of thread around any dc to mark Row 1 as **right** side.

Row 2: Ch 5 **(counts as first dc plus ch 2, now and throughout)**, turn; skip next ch-2 sp, dc in next dc **(1 beginning space made)**, (2 dc in next ch-2 sp, dc in next dc) 47 times **(47 blocks made)**, [ch 2, skip next ch-2 sp, dc in last dc **(1 space made)**]: 47 blocks and 2 spaces.

Row 3: Work beginning space, dc in next 15 dc **(5 blocks made)**, [ch 2, skip next 2 dc, dc in next dc **(1 space made)**], (work 5 blocks, work 1 space) 7 times: 40 blocks and 9 spaces.

Rows 4-141: Follow chart, pages 20 and 21.

Finish off.

Wash and block Table Runner *(see Washing and Blocking, page 31)*.

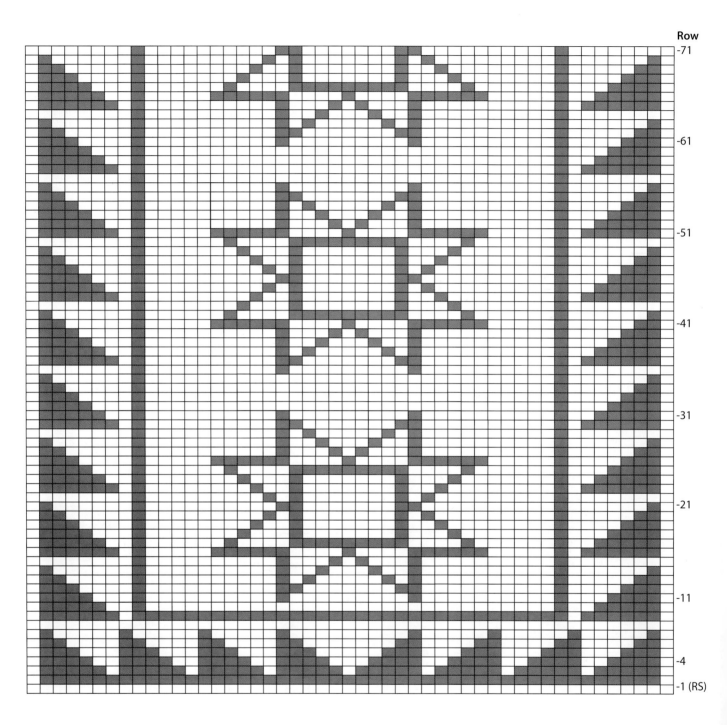

KEY

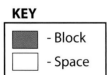

▨	- Block
☐	- Space

Row
-71
-61
-51
-41
-31
-21
-11
-4
-1 (RS)

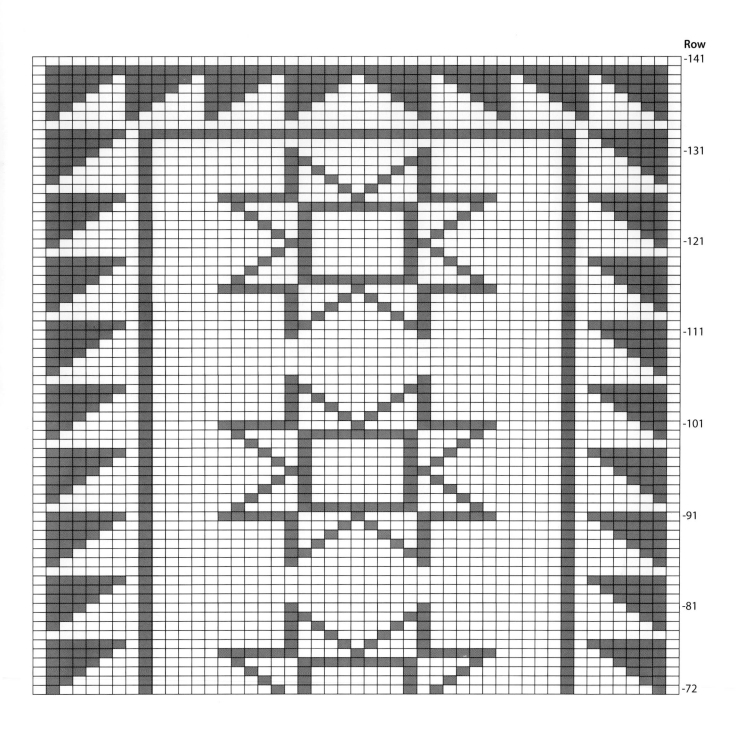

Row
-141
-131
-121
-111
-101
-91
-81
-72

Stars & Stripes

■■□□ **EASY +**

Approximate Finished Size: 14¼" wide x 30¾" long (36 cm x 78 cm) (excluding fringe)

SHOPPING LIST

Thread

(Bedspread Weight)

[400 yards (366 meters) per ball]:

☐ 3 balls

Crochet Hook

☐ Steel, size 7 (1.65 mm)

or size needed for gauge

GAUGE INFORMATION

20 dc and 10 rows = 2" (5 cm)

    9 spaces = 2" (5 cm) wide

Gauge Swatch: 2" (5 cm) square

Ch 22.

Row 1: Dc in fourth ch from hook
(3 skipped chs count as first dc) and
in each ch across: 20 dc.

Rows 2-10: Ch 3 **(counts as first dc)**,
turn; dc in next dc and in each dc
across.

Finish off.

INSTRUCTIONS
BODY

Ch 176.

Row 1: Dc in eighth ch from hook
**(7 skipped chs count as first dc plus
ch 2 and 2 skipped chs)**, ★ ch 2,
skip next 2 chs, dc in next ch; repeat
from ★ across: 58 dc and 57 ch-2 sps
(57 spaces).

Row 2 (Right side)**:** Ch 5 **(counts
as first dc plus ch 2, now and
throughout)**, turn; skip next ch-2 sp,
dc in next dc **(1 beginning space
made)**, (ch 2, skip next ch-2 sp, dc in
next dc) 18 times **(18 spaces made)**,
(2 dc in next ch-2 sp, dc in next
dc) 19 times **(19 blocks made)**, work
19 spaces: 38 spaces and 19 blocks.

Note: Loop a short piece of thread
around any dc to mark Row 2 as **right**
side.

Rows 3-6: Work beginning space,
work 18 spaces, dc in next 57 dc
(19 blocks made), work 19 spaces.

Row 7: Work beginning space, work
9 spaces, work 1 block, work 8 spaces,
work 10 blocks, [ch 2, skip next
2 dc, dc in next dc **(1 space made)**],
work 8 blocks, work 10 spaces, work
1 block, work 8 spaces: 20 blocks and
37 spaces.

Rows 8-39: Follow chart, page 24.

Rows 40-153: Following chart, repeat
Rows 2-39, 3 times.

Row 154: Work beginning space,
work 56 spaces; finish off.

Wash and block Table Runner *(see
Washing and Blocking, page 31)*

🎥 FRINGE

Cut a piece of cardboard 2" (5 cm) square. Wind the thread **loosely** and **evenly** around the cardboard until the card is filled, then cut across one end; repeat as needed.

Hold 4 strands together and fold in half.

With **wrong** side of short edge facing and using a crochet hook, draw the folded end up through a space and pull the loose ends through the folded end *(Fig. A)*; draw the knot up **tightly** *(Fig. B)*.

Repeat in each space across both short edges.

Lay Table Runner on a flat hard surface and trim fringe evenly.

Fig. A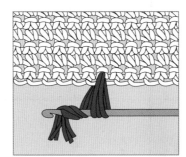

Fig. B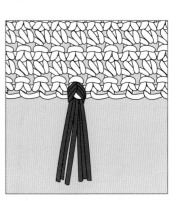

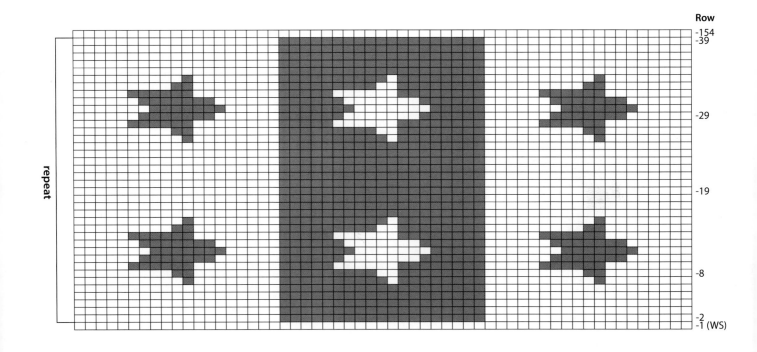

KEY

■	- Block
□	- Space

On **right** side rows, follow chart from **right** to **left**; on **wrong** side rows, follow chart from **left** to **right**.

Ziggy Zaggy

Shown on page 26.

■■□□ **EASY +**

Approximate Finished Size: 12½" wide x 29½" long (32 cm x 75 cm)

SHOPPING LIST

Thread

(Bedspread Weight)

[400 yards (366 meters) per ball]:

☐ 2 balls

Crochet Hook

☐ Steel, size 7 (1.65 mm)

or size needed for gauge

GAUGE INFORMATION

20 dc and 10 rows = 2" (5 cm)

9 spaces = 2" (5 cm) wide

Gauge Swatch: 2" (5 cm) square

Ch 22.

Row 1: Dc in fourth ch from hook **(3 skipped chs count as first dc)** and in each ch across: 20 dc.

Rows 2-10: Ch 3 **(counts as first dc)**, turn; dc in next dc and in each dc across.

Finish off.

INSTRUCTIONS
BODY

Ch 140.

Row 1 (Right side)**:** Dc in eighth ch from hook **(7 skipped chs count as first dc plus ch 2 and 2 skipped chs)**, ★ ch 2, skip next 2 chs, dc in next ch; repeat from ★ across: 46 dc and 45 ch-2 sps (45 spaces).

Note: Loop a short piece of thread around any dc to mark Row 1 as **right side.**

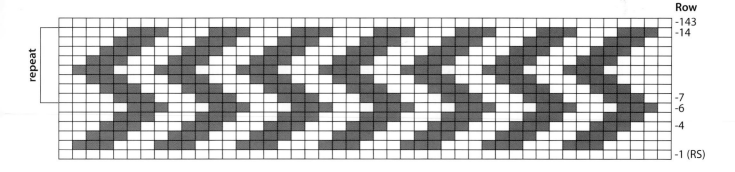

On **right** side rows, follow chart from **right** to **left**; on wrong side rows, follow chart from **left** to **right**.

KEY

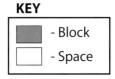

- Block

- Space

Row 2: Ch 5 (**counts as first dc plus ch 2, now and throughout**), turn; skip next ch-2 sp, dc in next dc (**1 beginning space made**), (2 dc in next ch-2 sp, dc in next dc) 3 times (**3 blocks made**), (ch 2, skip next ch-2 sp, dc in next dc) 3 times (**3 spaces made**), work 3 blocks, (work 3 spaces, work 3 blocks) 5 times, work 5 spaces: 24 spaces and 21 blocks.

Row 3: Work beginning space, work 3 spaces, work 1 block, dc in next 6 dc (**2 blocks made**), [ch 2, skip next 2 dc, dc in next dc (**1 space made**)], work 2 spaces, work 3 blocks, (work 3 spaces, work 3 blocks) 5 times, work 2 spaces.

Rows 4-6: Follow chart, page 25.

Rows 7-142: Following chart, repeat Rows 7-14, 17 times.

Row 143: Work beginning space, work 44 spaces; do **not** finish off.

BORDER

Border is worked in spaces around entire edge of Body.

Rnd 1: Ch 3 (**counts as first dc**), do **not** turn; working in sps at end of rows, 2 dc in first sp, † (ch 2, skip next sp, 3 dc in next sp) across, ch 3 (corner sp); working in sps across short edge, 3 dc in first sp, (ch 2, skip next sp, 3 dc in next sp) across, ch 3 (corner sp) †;

working in sps at end of rows, 3 dc in first sp, repeat from † to † once; join with slip st to first dc: 190 3-dc groups and 190 sps.

Rnd 2: Slip st in next 2 dc, ★ † [(slip st, ch 3, dc, ch 3, slip st) in next ch-2 sp, slip st in next 3 dc] across to corner ch-3 sp, slip st in corner sp, [ch 3, dc in same sp, ch 3, slip st in same sp] twice †, slip st in next 3 dc; repeat from ★ 2 times **more**, then repeat from † to † once; join with slip st to first slip st, finish off.

Wash and block Table Runner (*see Washing and Blocking, page 31*).

Pretty Pattern

Shown on page 29.

■■□□ EASY +

Approximate Finished Size: 13" wide x 30¼" long (33 cm x 77 cm)

SHOPPING LIST

Thread
(Bedspread Weight)

[400 yards (366 meters) per ball]:

☐ 2 balls

Crochet Hook

☐ Steel, size 7 (1.65 mm)

or size needed for gauge

GAUGE INFORMATION

20 dc and 10 rows = 2" (5 cm)

9 spaces = 2" (5 cm) wide

Gauge Swatch: 2" (5 cm) square

Ch 22.

Row 1: Dc in fourth ch from hook (**3 skipped chs count as first dc**) and in each ch across: 20 dc.

Rows 2-10: Ch 3 (**counts as first dc**), turn; dc in next dc and in each dc across.

Finish off.

INSTRUCTIONS
BODY

Ch 152.

Row 1: Dc in eighth ch from hook (**7 skipped chs count as first dc plus ch 2 and 2 skipped chs**), ★ ch 2, skip next 2 chs, dc in next ch; repeat from ★ across: 50 dc and 49 ch-2 sps (49 spaces).

Row 2 (Right side)**:** Ch 5 (**counts as first dc plus ch 2, now and throughout**), turn; skip next ch-2 sp, dc in next dc (**1 beginning space made**), (2 dc in next ch-2 sp, dc in next dc) 47 times (**47 blocks made**), [ch 2, skip next ch-2 sp, dc in last dc (**1 space made**)]: 47 blocks and 2 spaces.

Note: Loop a short piece of thread around any dc to mark Row 2 as **right** side.

Row 3: Work beginning space, [dc in next 3 dc (**1 block made**)], (ch 2, skip next 2 dc, dc in next dc) 3 times (**3 spaces made**), (work 3 blocks, work 3 spaces) 7 times, work 1 block, work 1 space: 26 spaces and 23 blocks.

Rows 4-47: Follow chart, page 28.

Rows 48-143: Following chart, repeat Rows 48-95 twice.

Rows 144-151: Follow chart.

Finish off.

Wash and block Table Runner *(see Washing and Blocking, page 31)*.

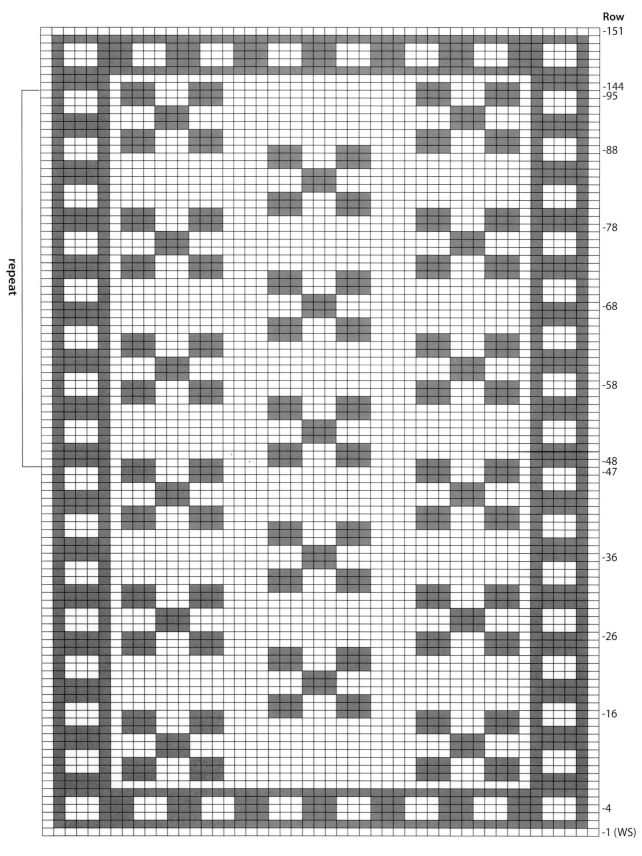

Row
-151
-144
-95
-88
-78
-68
-58
-48
-47
-36
-26
-16
-4
-1 (WS)

repeat

KEY

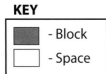

- Block
- Space

GENERAL INSTRUCTIONS

ABBREVIATIONS

ch(s)	chain(s)
cm	centimeters
dc	double crochet(s)
hdc	half double crochet(s)
mm	millimeters
Rnd(s)	Round(s)
RS	right side
sc	single crochet(s)
sp(s)	space(s)
st(s)	stitch(es)
tr	treble crochet(s)
WS	wrong side
YO	yarn over

SYMBOLS & TERMS

★ — work instructions following ★ as many **more** times as indicated in addition to the first time.

† to † — work all instructions from first † to second † **as many** times as specified.

( ) or [ ] — work enclosed instructions **as many** times as specified by the number immediately following **or** work all enclosed instructions in the stitch or space indicated **or** contains explanatory remarks.

colon (:) — the number(s) given after a colon at the end of a row or round denote(s) the number of stitches, blocks, or spaces you should have on that row or round.

GAUGE

Exact gauge is essential for proper size. Before beginning your project, make the sample swatch given in the individual instructions in the thread and hook specified. After completing the swatch, measure it, counting your stitches and rows carefully. If your swatch is larger or smaller than specified, **make another, changing hook size to get the correct gauge**. Keep trying until you find the size hook that will give you the specified gauge.

◖◻◻◻ BEGINNER	Projects for first-time crocheters using basic stitches. Minimal shaping.
◖◼◻◻ EASY	Projects using yarn with basic stitches, repetitive stitch patterns, simple color changes, and simple shaping and finishing.
◖◼◼◻ INTERMEDIATE	Projects using a variety of techniques, such as basic lace patterns or color patterns, mid-level shaping and finishing.
◖◼◼◼ EXPERIENCED	Projects with intricate stitch patterns, techniques and dimension, such as non-repeating patterns, multi-color techniques, fine threads, small hooks, detailed shaping and refined finishing.

STEEL CROCHET HOOKS															
U.S.	00	0	1	2	3	4	5	6	7	8	9	10	11	12	13	14
Metric - mm	3.5	3.25	2.75	2.25	2.1	2	1.9	1.8	1.65	1.5	1.4	1.3	1.1	1	.85	.75

FILET CROCHET TIP

To help achieve straight side edges, turn your work counterclockwise at the end of each row and work the last stitch in the back loop and back bar of the last dc (third chain of turning ch-3).

FREE LOOPS OF A CHAIN

When instructed to work in free loops of a chain, work in loop indicated by arrow (Fig. 1).

Fig. 1

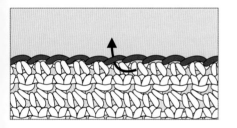

WASHING

Despite the fragile appearance of threadwork, it is very durable and can last a lifetime with proper care. Always wash the item when you finish crocheting it. The thread undergoes a lot of handling during construction and the oils from your hands can soil the work. Washing and blocking helps to "set" the stitches resulting in a neat and uniform appearance and giving your work a "professional" look. Using a mild detergent and warm water (never hot!), gently squeeze suds through the piece. Being careful not to rub, twist or wring, rinse the piece several times in cool, clear water. Roll it in an absorbent towel and gently press out the excess moisture.

BLOCKING

After washing the design and while it is still wet, place it on a blocking board, an ironing board, or a piece of cardboard covered with a towel. Pin the design to the size indicated in the individual instructions with rustproof pins. Make sure that all of the stitches and rows in the design are straight. Allow the design to dry completely.

CROCHET TERMINOLOGY	
UNITED STATES	**INTERNATIONAL**
slip stitch (slip st) =	single crochet (sc)
single crochet (sc) =	double crochet (dc)
half double crochet (hdc) =	half treble crochet (htr)
double crochet (dc) =	treble crochet(tr)
treble crochet (tr) =	double treble crochet (dtr)
double treble crochet (dtr) =	triple treble crochet (ttr)
triple treble crochet (tr tr) =	quadruple treble crochet (qtr)
skip =	miss

Yarn Weight Symbol & Names	LACE 0	SUPER FINE 1	FINE 2	LIGHT 3	MEDIUM 4	BULKY 5	SUPER BULKY 6
Type of Yarns in Category	Fingering, 10-count crochet thread	Sock, Fingering Baby	Sport, Baby	DK, Light Worsted	Worsted, Afghan, Aran	Chunky, Craft, Rug	Bulky, Roving
Crochet Gauge* Ranges in Single Crochet to 4" (10 cm)	32-42 double crochets**	21-32 sts	16-20 sts	12-17 sts	11-14 sts	8-11 sts	5-9 sts
Advised Hook Size Range	Steel*** 6,7,8 Regular hook B-1	B-1 to E-4	E-4 to 7	7 to I-9	I-9 to K-10.5	K-10.5 to M-13	M-13 and larger

*GUIDELINES ONLY: The chart above reflects the most commonly used gauges and hook sizes for specific yarn categories.

** Lace weight yarns are usually crocheted on larger-size hooks to create lacy openwork patterns. Accordingly, a gauge range is difficult to determine. Always follow the gauge stated in your pattern.

*** Steel crochet hooks are sized differently from regular hooks–the higher the number the smaller the hook, which is the reverse of regular hook sizing.

MEET JOYCE GEISLER

Joyce Geisler learned to crochet around the age of 14. Taught by her grandmother and aunt, she developed a love for working with thread and crocheting doilies. Today, Joyce and her husband, Rick, have a grain farm and small trucking company in Maryland.

Joyce says, "I find that crochet is an excellent way to relax at the end of a long day." This includes designing patterns in filet crochet depicting their day-to-day life on the farm. With inspiration coming from everyday things such as floor tiles or fabric patterns, Joyce developed the runners in this book and many other lovely designs. Another favorite way that Joyce and Rick spend their free time is enjoying the company of their grandchildren, Addie and Charlie.

For a peek inside Joyce's crocheting world, visit her blog at www.thefarmerswifecrochet.blogspot.com.

THREAD INFORMATION

Each Table Runner in this book was made using Aunt Lydia's Classic Crochet Cotton Thread, size10 (color #0001 White). Any brand of bedspread weight cotton thread may be used. It is best to refer to the yardage/meters when determining how many balls to purchase. Remember, to arrive at the finished size, it is the GAUGE/TENSION that is important, not the brand of thread.

We have made every effort to ensure that these instructions are accurate and complete. We cannot, however, be responsible for human error, typographical mistakes, or variations in individual work.

Production Team: Technical Editor/Writer - Linda A. Daley; Editorial Writer - Susan Frantz Wiles; Senior Graphic Artist - Lora Puls; Graphic Artist - Kara Darling and Becca Snider Tally; Photo Stylist - Lori Wenger; and Photographer - Jason Masters.